MARTIN LUTHER KING, Jr.

by Margaret Holland, Ph.D.
illustrated by Dick Smolinski

For David

Published by Worthington Press
10100 SBF Drive, Pinellas Park, Florida 34666

Printed in the United States of America

10 9 8 7 6 5 4 3 2

ISBN 0-87406-507-0

Contents

Chapter One

Growing Up

Fourteen-year-old M.L. King would never forget the day he gave his speech on the Negro and the Constitution. M.L. won second place in a public speaking contest. Afterward, M.L. and his teacher were riding home, happily talking about the day. Then some white passengers climbed aboard the bus, and the driver ordered M.L. and his teacher to give up their seats. When M.L. didn't move, the driver swore at him. His teacher, Mrs. Bradley, urged M.L. to move. She said it was the law. And so, M.L. and Mrs. Bradley had to stand in the aisle for 90 miles, all the way from Valdosta back to Atlanta, Georgia. King said of the experience, "That night will never leave my memory. It was the angriest I have ever been in my life."

But what happened on the bus that night was not new for Martin Luther King, Jr. As a black child born in Atlanta in 1929, he was often treated differently from white children because of segregation. Segregation laws kept blacks

apart from whites. Black children did not attend the same schools as white children. Blacks couldn't swim in the pools where whites swam or play in the parks where whites played. Blacks were not allowed to sleep in the same hotels or eat in the same restaurants as whites. On sidewalks, blacks were expected to step aside for whites, and on buses, blacks had to give up their seats for whites.

M.L. first began learning about racial discrimination and segregation when he was five. He used to play with two white boys who lived near him. One day, the boys' parents

told M.L. to go away. M.L. wanted to know why. The parents said, "Because we are white and you are colored."

When M.L. returned home, he cried and told his mother what had happened. Then his mother knew she had to explain about slavery and racial discrimination and segregation. She told him how blacks had been captured in Africa and taken to the United States and other countries to be the slaves of the white people. She told him of how President Abraham Lincoln had freed the slaves.

Martin's mother told him to keep his head up. "You

must never feel that you are less than anybody else," she told him. "You must always feel that you are somebody."

Martin Luther King, Jr., was called M.L. by his friends and family because he and his father had the same name. M.L.'s father, Martin Luther King, Sr., was a leader in the black community and an educated man. Daddy King, as everyone called Martin Luther King, Sr., had spent 11 years working during the day and studying at night to get his high school diploma. During the time he was working and studying in Atlanta, he met Alberta Williams, a school teacher who was the daughter of the Reverend Adam Daniel Williams, pastor of the Ebenezer Baptist Church. Martin Luther King, Sr., was already a preacher. But to become a leader in the church, he needed a degree in theology, which is the study of God and religion.

Finally, he was admitted to Morehouse College. That same year, he married Alberta and became her father's assistant at the Ebenezer Baptist Church. When M.L. was two years old, the Reverend Williams died, and Daddy King became pastor of the church.

M.L. saw that whites insulted his father even though his father was the pastor of a church. One day, his father took him downtown to buy him a pair of shoes. They went into a store and sat near the front. When the clerk appeared, he told them he would wait on them if they would move to the back of the store.

"We'll either buy shoes sitting right here, or we won't buy shoes at all," the Reverend King declared angrily.

Then he took M.L. by the hand and walked out of the store. Outside he looked at his son and said, "I don't care how long I have to live with this system, I'll never accept it."

Young M.L. was always a good student. He skipped a grade in elementary school and started high school when he was 13. When he was 15, M.L. applied to Morehouse College. He passed the entrance exam and was allowed to skip his last year of high school.

The summer before he started college, M.L. left the segregated South for the first time. He took a summer job in Connecticut working on a tobacco farm. When M.L. went into the city of Hartford, he could walk in any park, eat in any restaurant, and sit anywhere he chose in the movies. At home, M.L. had to sit in a segregated balcony to see a movie. At the end of the summer, when M.L. caught the train in Hartford, he sat where he liked.

But when the train entered the South, suddenly the rules changed. When he went to the dining car, M.L. was led to a table in the rear. There the waiter pulled a curtain down around him so that the whites would not see him.

Chapter Two

College and Courtship

Daddy King wanted his son to follow him into the ministry and become his assistant. But when he entered Morehouse in 1944, 15-year-old M.L. thought he wanted to be a doctor.

M.L. learned about the black leaders who had worked against racism. He began developing his own ideas about how blacks could gain equality with whites. Then Dr. Benjamin Mays, the president of Morehouse, began to help M.L. see the role of a minister differently. Mays believed the church should support black rights and work for racial equality. By the time he was 18, Martin Luther King had decided to be a minister.

During the summers while M.L. was in college, he worked as a laborer. When one foreman kept calling him "nigger," he quit his job. He also realized that most poor blacks couldn't afford to do that, and he learned that blacks made lower wages than whites for doing the same jobs.

During 1948, his senior year, he wrote an article for the school newspaper. He criticized students who were not using their educations to help fellow blacks. Also that year, on February 25, 19-year-old Martin Luther King, Jr., was ordained as a minister and made Assistant Pastor at Ebenezer Baptist Church.

When he graduated from Morehouse in June of 1948, King applied and was admitted to Crozer Theological Seminary in Chester, Pennsylvania. For the first time, M.L. was attending an integrated school. He was worried

that the whites might think all blacks were lazy and sloppy. He dressed neatly, kept his room spotless, and studied so hard that he earned straight A's. When he realized that he was being accepted as an equal, M.L. began to relax and enjoy Crozer. And even though he continued to make top grades, he found time to have fun.

One evening, M.L. attended a lecture about Mahatma Gandhi, the man who had led the Indian people in their struggle for independence from Great Britain. Gandhi had taught the people to stage peaceful protests and use love and nonviolence to end oppression. He believed that hatred only created more hatred. He led them in nonviolent boycotts, marches, and strikes. He taught them to go to jail

willingly after they refused to follow unjust laws.

Gandhi had been assassinated in 1948, but King saw how Gandhi's work had won freedom for the people of India. King began to see a way for black Americans to end segregation.

In 1951, Martin Luther King, Jr., graduated from Crozer Seminary. He had been president of the student body during his senior year. As a top graduate in his class, he received a $1,300 scholarship to continue his studies. Daddy King wanted his son to return to Atlanta and assist him at Ebenezer Church, but M.L. wanted to earn a doctorate in religion. Daddy King gave in and M.L. left for graduate school at Boston University.

In Boston, King continued to study hard. He met Coretta Scott. Coretta had grown up on a farm in Alabama and won a scholarship to Antioch College in Ohio. Now she was studying to become a classical singer. King was ready to marry, and he saw that Coretta had all the qualities he wanted in a wife—character, intelligence, personality, and beauty.

But Daddy King wanted his son to marry someone from Atlanta. Besides, Coretta was two years older than M.L., and she was a farmer's daughter. But M.L. was determined to marry Coretta. Finally, Daddy King gave in. On June 18,

1953, Daddy King conducted their wedding ceremony.

After their marriage, the newlyweds continued their studies in Boston. When Coretta had finished her degree, King was ready to begin preaching. Daddy King begged M.L. to come back to Ebenezer, but M.L. wanted a church of his own. Coretta wanted to stay in the North, but King wanted to find a church in the South. "I'm going to live in the South because that's where I'm needed," he told Coretta.

Chapter Three

Montgomery

On September 1, 1954, M.L. and Coretta King arrived in Montgomery, Alabama. King had been chosen as the new minister of the Dexter Avenue Baptist Church. A few months earlier, the U.S. Supreme Court had ruled that school segregation was unconstitutional. Many whites were furious.

Montgomery was a segregated city of 10,000 whites and 50,000 blacks. Most of the blacks lived in old, run-down houses without electricity or running water. Very few blacks owned cars. They depended on the city buses. King urged his church members to resist segregation. Another Baptist minister in Montgomery, Ralph Abernathy, was preaching the same thing. Soon King and the Reverend Abernathy became close friends. For the rest of King's life, they would work together against segregation.

In 1955, Coretta gave birth to their first born, a girl named Yolanda Denise (or Yoki for short). Just after Yoki

was born, something happened in Montgomery that was to set the direction for King's life. A seamstress named Rosa Parks was arrested for refusing to give her bus seat to a white man. When Montgomery's black leaders heard what had happened, they decided to ask blacks to boycott the buses on the Monday of Mrs. Parks's trial.

They passed out thousands of leaflets. On Sunday, black pastors announced the boycott in their churches. The next day the buses in Montgomery were almost completely empty. Almost no blacks rode the bus.

Rosa Parks was found guilty of breaking a state segregation law and fined ten dollars. She appealed the verdict. The same day, the black leaders of Montgomery met to plan how they could continue the boycott. They formed the Montgomery Improvement Association, the M.I.A., and they elected Dr. King as their president.

That evening King gave his first major protest speech to thousands of blacks. "We are here this evening to say to those who have mistreated us so long that we are tired, tired of being segregated and humiliated...Love must be our ideal...We must not end up hating our white brothers."

When he sat down, the crowd cheered. The blacks of Montgomery decided to continue the boycott until the bus company agreed that drivers would stop insulting black passengers and would allow passengers to sit anywhere. King thought that these were reasonable proposals, but the white leaders rejected them all.

The M.I.A. organized a car pool so that riders were driven to their jobs and back home. The blacks held meetings in the black churches. And night after night, King explained the principles of love and nonviolence.

The whites despised what King was doing. Angry whites threatened him and called him "nigger." On January 30, 1956, almost two months after the boycott had

started, King's home was bombed. He was away at a meeting, but Coretta and Yoki were in the back of the house. Fortunately, Coretta and Yoki were safe.

When King arrived home, an angry crowd of blacks was gathered in front of his house. Some had knives and guns. King went out on the damaged porch and told them to go home and put away their weapons. "I want you to love our enemies," he urged. Slowly the people quieted down and left. King had been true to the principles of nonviolence. He had prevented what could have become a horrible race riot.

Month after month the boycott continued. King and other leaders of the M.I.A. were arrested, tried, and found guilty of breaking segregation laws. Lawyers for the M.I.A. appealed the convictions and began a lawsuit to have the city's segregation law declared unconstitutional. The N.A.A.C.P. (National Association for the Advancement of Colored People) had already filed suit in federal court. And on November 13, 1956, the U.S. Supreme Court declared Alabama's state and local laws requiring segregation on buses to be unconstitutional.

King and the M.I.A. had won, but King knew that violence was still a danger. He worked hard training the black bus riders in nonviolent responses. If they were cursed at, they were not to curse back. If they were hit, they were not to strike back. If they saw someone else being attacked, they were not to help that person. Instead, they were to pray for the people doing the attacking. One week after the buses were desegregated, angry whites attacked and overturned some buses. There was no violence in return. The blacks stayed true to King's "love power" philosophy. In time, Montgomery quieted down and the buses were integrated.

Chapter Four

Spreading the Word

The Montgomery bus boycott changed things for many blacks. For the first time, blacks working by themselves had peacefully overcome segregation. King received invitations to speak from all over the country. People everywhere—black and white—wanted to know about him. His picture appeared on the front cover of Time magazine. King responded by writing a book, *Stride Toward Freedom,* about what had happened in Montgomery.

In September, 1958, King was autographing copies of his book at a bookstore in Harlem. Suddenly, a black woman in the crowd came up to him and stabbed him with a razor-sharp letter opener. King was taken to a Harlem hospital where surgeons had to cut out one of his ribs to remove the blade from his chest. The blade was so close to his heart that if he had moved, or even sneezed, he might have died. While he was in the hospital, King received a letter from a ninth-grade white girl. She wrote, "I read that if you had sneezed, you would have died. I'm simply writing you to say that I'm so happy that you didn't sneeze."

People were amazed when King asked that the woman who attacked him not be charged. She was later committed to a hospital for the mentally ill. While he was recovering from the wound, Martin and Coretta took a trip to India to see the land of Gandhi. King returned more committed than ever to nonviolence.

Earlier, King and his friend Abernathy had joined other Southern black ministers to form the Southern Christian Leadership Conference (SCLC). King was the president, and Abernathy was the treasurer. In December, 1959, King resigned as the pastor of the Dexter Avenue Baptist Church in order to devote more time to working for the SCLC. He, Coretta, Yoki, and his son Martin Luther King III, moved to Atlanta. Daddy King was delighted to have his son as assistant at Ebenezer, but King knew that his real work was to push on in the struggle against segregation.

At that time, blacks were not allowed to eat in many restaurants and lunch counters. They were also forbidden to use the same rest rooms as whites. In February, 1960, four black students in Greensboro, North Carolina, sat down at a lunch counter in a Woolworth's store. They said that they would not leave until they were served.

Soon, all over the South, black students, often with whites helping them, were "sitting in" at lunch counters. The biggest sit-in occurred in Nashville, Tennessee. Over 500 students staged a demonstration for integrated lunch counters, movies, and public rest room facilities. During the demonstration, they began singing an old labor union song, "We Shall Overcome." The song eventually became the theme song of the civil rights movement during the 1960s.

As the sit-ins continued, the SCLC invited the student leaders to a meeting in North Carolina. The students formed a group called the Student Nonviolent Coordinating Committee (SNCC)—or SNICK as it was usually called. SNCC was not a part of the SCLC, but Martin Luther King, Jr., was the guiding force in both organizations.

Soon SNCC leaders began planning a campaign of sit-ins in Atlanta. Daddy King and the older leaders of the black community who had been working patiently to desegregate Atlanta were opposed to the campaign. Martin didn't want to defy his father, but he realized that he had to support the students.

On October 19, 1960, King and a group of students sat down at a whites-only restaurant in Rich's Department Store in Atlanta. They were arrested for trespassing and

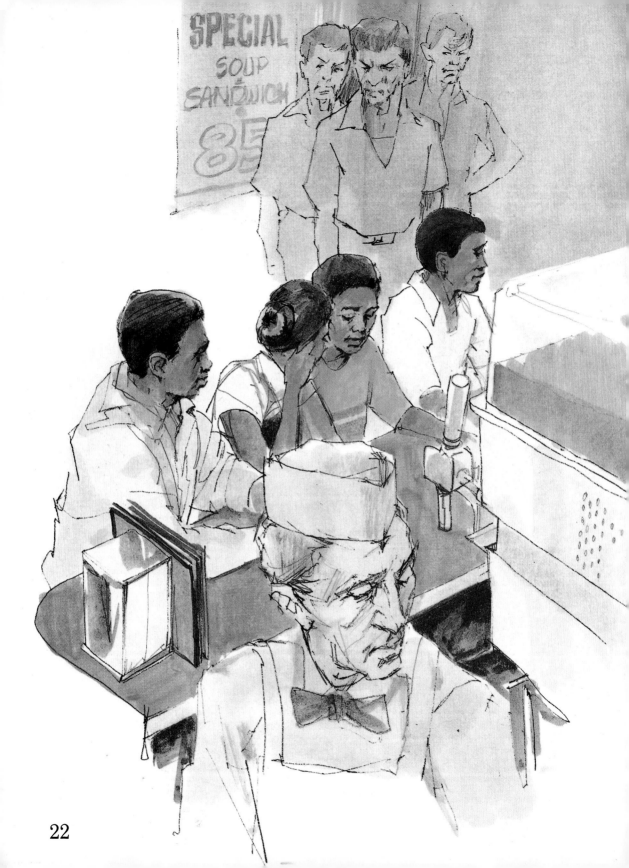

22

taken to jail. All except King were quickly released.

Earlier that year, King had been arrested for driving on an expired driver's license. He had been fined 25 dollars and had been placed on a year's probation. Now county officials used this new arrest to say that he had broken the terms of his probation, and a local judge quickly found King guilty. The judge sentenced him to four months of hard labor in a state prison. In the middle of the night, he was transferred to a cell for violent criminals in a penitentiary that was known for abusing blacks.

What King didn't know was that his being sentenced to prison was becoming a factor in the national elections. In 1960, Democratic Senator John F. Kennedy was running against Republican Vice President Richard M. Nixon for president of the United States. When the news media released the story of what had happened to Martin Luther King, Jr., Nixon did nothing. But Kennedy acted.

Senator Kennedy himself called Coretta King to express his concern for her husband. Then he had his brother and campaign manager, Robert Kennedy, call the judge in the case. Robert Kennedy was outraged by what had happened. He urged that King be released on bail immediately. The next day the judge reopened the case and allowed King to be released on two thousand dollars bond.

When King arrived home, he announced to the media that he was "indebted" to Senator Kennedy for making his release possible.

Blacks all over the country were impressed. They had not expected a white politician to do anything like what Senator Kennedy did. Daddy King, who had been planning to vote for Nixon, announced from his pulpit at Ebenezer Church that he was now supporting Kennedy. And the Reverend Abernathy urged blacks to take off their Nixon buttons.

No one can know whether enough people changed their vote over the King issue to make Kennedy the winner. But Kennedy won the election by a very, very small number of votes. One well-known Republican told reporters that Kennedy had won because he had made "a couple of phone calls." As soon as he was in office, President Kennedy appointed his brother Robert to the office of Attorney General. Martin Luther King, Jr., and other black leaders hoped the Kennedys would help blacks finally have the rights that the Constitution guaranteed them.

Chapter Five

Birmingham

When King's daughter Yoki was six years old, she saw a TV commercial for a new amusement park in Atlanta. She wanted to go. At first her parents made excuses, but Yoki continued to beg to go. Finally her mother had to tell her the truth. The park was only for whites. King often talked about that experience in his speeches. He told how hard it was to explain to Yoki why she couldn't go. And he told how he had promised her that someday she would be able to go there or any other place that she chose.

In 1962, King, Abernathy, and other leaders in the SCLC decided to start a campaign against segregation in Birmingham, Alabama. Birmingham was the largest manufacturing city in the South. It was also completely segregated. George Wallace, the new governor of Alabama, had vowed that in Alabama there would be segregation forever. The police department was led by Commissioner Bull Connor. Connor had promised that blood would flow

before there would be any integration in Birmingham.

The SCLC leaders wanted integration of downtown lunch counters, rest rooms, and drinking fountains, and more jobs for blacks. They planned to use boycotts and mass marches to focus attention on the issues. After the first day of protest, the city obtained a ruling from the state court forbidding any more marches or protests. But King and several others decided to march anyway.

On Good Friday, April 13, 1963, King and Abernathy led about 50 people toward the downtown stores. When they met Bull Connor and the police, King and Abernathy knelt in prayer. The police immediately arrested them and the other protesters. King spent nine days in jail in isolation, separated from the other protesters. During that time, he wrote his famous "Letter From a Birmingham Jail." He explained his reasons for disobeying unjust laws and restated the purpose of the protest.

When King was released, he found that adult blacks were afraid to join the marches for fear of losing their jobs. But other leaders had been teaching the students of the city the principles of nonviolent protest. The youngsters wanted to march. At first King and the other leaders said no. Then they realized that unless they let the children march, the protest would be defeated.

On May 2, a thousand black children, ages 6 to 16, marched toward downtown Birmingham. About 900 were arrested. The next day, 2,500 children marched. When they turned a corner, the marchers were met by firemen holding high-pressure hoses and police holding snarling dogs ready to attack. Bull Connor yelled at them to turn back. But then Connor ordered the firemen to turn their high-pressure hoses on and force the children back.

Hard streams of water knocked the children to the sidewalks and pushed them against the walls. Black bystanders began throwing rocks at the firemen and police. Then Connor ordered the police dogs to attack. That night, people across the country were shocked when the TV news showed black children in Birmingham being attacked. President Kennedy said that the pictures coming from Birmingham made him sick.

Again, the next day and the next, the children marched in spite of the hoses and dogs, in spite of their fears. And they were arrested. More than 3,000 children had been jailed.

On Sunday, May 5, another 3,000 children began marching toward the jail to pray for the ones who had been arrested. The marchers knelt in prayer. One of the leaders said, "Turn on your water. Turn loose your dogs. We will stand here till we die." The blacks waited. Connor ordered the hoses turned on, but nothing happened. Slowly the policemen and firemen stepped aside and let the marchers through. To the marchers it seemed like a miracle! The news media showed the scene to Americans everywhere—an ugly, violent, racist white police commissioner and the nonviolent, well-disciplined young blacks.

May 7 was to be the biggest march of all. Thousands of children coming in from all directions reached the middle of town. Once again the hoses and dogs were used to push the children back.

The business leaders were horrified by what was happening. They were disgusted with Bull Connor. They began serious negotiations to end the conflict. After hours and hours, they reached an agreement. Within 90 days, drinking fountains, rest rooms, and lunch counters would be desegregated. Within 60 days, blacks would be hired in sales and clerical positions. And everyone who had been arrested would be released.

At last, blacks had broken through the walls of segregation in the South's toughest city. And they had done it by using King's nonviolent methods.

Chapter Six

"I Have a Dream"

Two days after the Birmingham agreement was reached, angry whites bombed the motel where King had been staying. The whites also bombed his brother's home in Birmingham. The bombing started a riot. King was deeply upset by the violence. He returned to help calm the people, but President Kennedy had to send federal troops into Birmingham to quiet the city.

One month after the Birmingham riot, the President, in a nationally televised speech, proposed a strong law barring segregation in all public places. In his speech, Kennedy reminded people that even though Abraham Lincoln had freed the slaves 100 years before, blacks were not really free. King and others began planning a huge march in Washington, D.C., to help support Kennedy's bill.

On August 28, 1963, 250,000 people turned out for one of the largest demonstrations in U.S. history. At the Lincoln Memorial, Martin Luther King, Jr., was intro-

duced. He looked out across the crowd. He began slowly and then caught fire: "I have a dream that one day on the red hills of Georgia, the sons of former slaves and the sons of slave owners will be able to sit down together at the table of brotherhood...I have a dream that my four little children will one day live in a nation where they will be judged, not by the color of their skin, but by the content of their character."

The crowd cheered as he continued. "When we let freedom ring...we will be able to speed up that day when all of God's children will be able to join hands and sing in the words of the old Negro spiritual, 'Free at last! Free at last! Thank God Almighty we are free at last!'"

But King's dream was a long time away. Soon violence erupted again. A month after the march, four young black girls were killed when a bomb was thrown into the Sixteenth Street Baptist Church in Birmingham. And on November 22, 1963, Kennedy was assassinated. King and his wife watched TV as the story of Kennedy's death unfolded. "This is what is going to happen to me also," he told his wife. "I don't think I can survive either."

Kennedy's successor was Lyndon B. Johnson, a Southerner. Would he support Kennedy's bill? In his first speech to Congress, the new president urged

passage of Kennedy's civil rights bill. On July 2, 1964, Johnson signed the Civil Rights Act into law. Martin Luther King, Jr., stood behind him as the president signed. Now, motels, restaurants, and movies had to admit blacks. Discrimination in business was illegal. But the law said nothing about voting rights or housing.

In October, Martin Luther King, Jr., won the Nobel Prize for Peace. It is one of the most famous awards in the world. In December, King and his family flew to Norway to accept the award. In his acceptance speech,

King said "This Award...is a profound recognition that nonviolence is the answer to the crucial political and social questions of our time." When he returned to the U.S., King was greeted with a hero's welcome.

But back in the South, there was still much work to be done. Very few blacks were registered to vote. White officials used all kinds of tricks to prevent blacks from registering. They gave blacks impossibly difficult tests. They closed registration lines when blacks appeared. And they used force and terror to keep blacks from voting. For their voting rights campaign, King and the SCLC leaders chose Selma, Alabama. In Selma, only 383 blacks had managed to register to vote out of the 15,000 blacks who were eligible.

For seven weeks people were arrested and jailed as the marches continued. King and Abernathy were arrested again and spent four days in jail. Then King decided that the marchers would walk from Selma to Montgomery, the capital of Alabama. They would present their case to Governor George Wallace. But Wallace was determined to prevent the march. On Sunday, March 7, with King in Atlanta, 500 people began the march out of Selma. The marchers walked to the bridge on the outside of town. At the far end of the bridge, state troopers and local police blocked the way. The marchers were told to go back; they paused. Then the police charged. They beat the marchers back with bullwhips, clubs, and tear gas.

Again, TV cameras recorded it all. Horrified Americans saw troopers on horseback using bullwhips on people who were trying to escape. In Atlanta, an upset King spoke on national television, asking ministers and others to come to Selma to join him in the next march. Two days later, King led 1,500 marchers out of Selma. When they faced the police at the end of the bridge, they knelt and

37

prayed. Then King had them turn around. He wanted to prevent more violence. Many black leaders criticized King, calling him a traitor and a coward. But King was determined to prevent more injuries and possible deaths.

More violence came anyway. Reverend James Reed, a white minister from Boston, was beaten so badly in Selma that he died two days later. People all over the country were angry. Demonstrators in many cities protested the violence in Selma. Four thousand religious leaders protested in Washington, calling for action from the president. On March 15, 1965, President Johnson appeared on prime-time television to ask Congress to pass a voting rights law. On August 6, 1965, he signed the bill into law. The 1965 Voting Rights Act outlawed the difficult tests and gave the Attorney General power to appoint more people to register those who were being kept off the list of voters. Immediately blacks in the South, especially in Alabama, began registering to vote in large numbers.

The Selma campaign was probably Martin Luther King's greatest triumph because the 1965 Voting Rights Act was a direct result of the actions there.

Chapter Seven

"Free at Last"

Segregation was now legally dead in the South and throughout the U.S. But many blacks were angry because they still didn't have the opportunities that whites did. Many disagreed with Martin Luther King's nonviolent approach. As early as 1963, a black leader named Malcolm X was advising blacks to overthrow white power, to use violence to replace white power with black power.

Only five days after President Johnson signed the Voting Rights Act, violence broke out in a neighborhood of Los Angeles called Watts. In six days of looting and rioting, 34 people were killed and over 600 were injured. King was horrified when, watching on TV, he saw young blacks yelling, "Burn, baby, burn!"

The next summer James Meredith, who, four years earlier, had been the first black admitted to the University of Mississippi, was shot and wounded by a white. He had been on a one-man voter registration march at the time.

40

King and other black leaders rushed to Mississippi to stage the "James Meredith March Against Fear." But Stokely Carmichael, the new chairman of SNCC, did not accept King's nonviolent approach. At rallies, Carmichael led the people in chanting "Black Power!" When King asked the group not to use the "Black Power" slogan, they refused.

During the summers of 1966 and 1967, there were riots in the ghettos of several northern cities. Blacks in the North often suffered racial discrimination in their search for jobs and housing. They had to live in dangerous run-down neighborhoods called ghettos.

King was opposed to all violence. In 1967, he spoke out against the war in Vietnam. A *Life* magazine editorial declared that by connecting "civil rights with...Vietnam, King comes close to betraying the cause for which he has worked so long." Many black leaders agreed.

King was tired and depressed. Sometimes he felt that everyone was attacking him and his beliefs. Early in 1968, King received a call from Memphis, Tennessee. The Memphis garbage collectors, who were almost all blacks, were striking. The city refused to negotiate with them. They needed King's help.

On March 28, 1968, King and Abernathy led a march

toward the Memphis city hall. Suddenly they heard glass shattering. A gang of black teenagers was throwing rocks, smashing windows, and yelling, "Black Power!" King was determined that he would never lead a violent march. He and Abernathy got into a car and returned to their motel.

They watched on TV as the riot continued. When it was over, one teenager was dead, killed by police. Sixty people were injured, and 155 stores were damaged. King returned to Atlanta, more depressed than ever. But he was determined to stage another march in Memphis, this time a peaceful one.

His chance came on April 3. King returned and gave

a speech at the Masonic Temple in Memphis. At the end of his speech he said, "It doesn't really matter what happens now...because I have been to the mountaintop. Like anybody, I'd like to live a long life...but I'm not concerned about that now, I just want to do God's will."

Twenty-four hours later, 39-year-old Martin Luther King, Jr., was dead. An assassin had shot him while he was standing on the balcony of his motel. His killer was a white man who hated blacks.

People will always remember Martin Luther King's message of nonviolence and his dream of racial equality. In many parts of the world, there is still much racism and violence. But Martin Luther King's life showed that even the oldest hatreds can be overcome. That is why people all over the world are grateful to Dr. King. They consider him a great hero.

So in 1983, the Congress of the United States created a federal holiday honoring Dr. King. The third Monday of January every year is set aside as Martin Luther King Day. He is the only individual to have a national holiday in his honor. George Washington and Abraham Lincoln share the holiday called Presidents' Day.

At the ceremony to establish this new holiday, President Ronald Reagan said that Dr. King's life "symbolized what was right about America, what was noblest and best." And King's wife, Coretta Scott King, urged people everywhere to carry on his dream of racial equality.

Today Martin Luther King's message of nonviolence in all things, and his dream of equality for all, are goals still to be strived for until everyone everywhere is "free at last."

Time Line

1929   Martin Luther King, Jr., born in Atlanta, Georgia.

1944   M.L. admitted to Morehouse College.

1948   February 25—King ordained as a minister.

  June—King admitted to Crozer Theological Seminary.

  Mahatma Gandhi assassinated.

1951   King graduates from Crozer and wins scholarship to Boston University.

1953   June 18—King marries Coretta Scott.

1954   Supreme Court outlaws school segregation.

  September 1—Kings arrive in Montgomery, Alabama. King begins work as new minister for Dexter Avenue Baptist Church.

1955   King receives Doctor of Philosophy degree.

  King leads boycott against Montgomery bus company.

1956   January 30—King home bombed.

  November 13—U.S. Supreme Court rules segregation on buses unconstitutional.

1958   September—King stabbed at bookstore in Harlem.

1959   December—Family moves to Atlanta, where King becomes his father's assistant at the Ebenezer Baptist Church. King also serves as SCLC president.

1960   February—First sit-in, Greensboro, North Carolina.

  October 19—King arrested in Atlanta. Senator John F. Kennedy, a candidate for president, helps get King released.

  November—Kennedy wins presidential election.

1962   King and other SCLC leaders start campaign against segregation in Birmingham, Alabama.

1963	April 13—First march on Birmingham. King arrested. King writes "Letter from a Birmingham Jail."
	May 2—First children's march in Birmingham. Many children arrested and jailed.
	May 5—Police and firemen let marchers pass. Birmingham leaders finally agree to end segregation. Two days later, motel where King stayed is bombed.
	June—President Kennedy proposes passage of anti-segregation law.
	August 28—King delivers "I Have a Dream" speech.
	November 22—President Kennedy assassinated. King tells his wife that he thinks he will be shot, too.
	December—King accepts Nobel Peace Prize.
1964	President Johnson signs Civil Rights Act. Martin Luther King stands behind Johnson at ceremony.
1965	January 2—King announces SCLC campaign to win voting rights in Selma, Alabama. Marches begin in Selma and people are jailed during the seven weeks.
	March 7—First attempt to march from Selma to Montgomery. Police attack marchers.
	March 9—Second march to Montgomery. King turns march around to avoid violence. Later, white minister James Reed is beaten and killed.
	August 6—President Johnson signs Voting Rights Act. Five days later, rioting breaks out in black neighborhood of Los Angeles.
1966-67	Blacks riot in ghettos of several northern cities. Vietnam war continues. King speaks against the war.
1968	April 3—King leads peaceful march in Memphis. Twenty-four hours later, King is assassinated.
1983	U.S. Congress establishes federal holiday honoring Dr. Martin Luther King, Jr.

Glossary

boycott Refusing to have dealings with a person or place to show disapproval or to get people to accept certain conditions.

civil rights The rights of personal freedom guaranteed to U.S. citizens by the U.S. Constitution and by acts of Congress.

demonstration A public display of group feelings toward a person or cause.

discrimination Prejudiced outlook, action, or treatment based on something other than a person's merit.

integration Different groups, such as races, coming together as equals.

Nobel Prize An award given for the encouragement of persons who work for the interests of humanity.

nonviolent protest Demonstrations that are free from violence.

racism Judging people by the color of their skin.

riot A noisy, violent public disorder caused by a group or crowd of persons protesting against something.

segregation The separation or isolation of a race, class, or ethnic group by discriminatory means.

sit-in The act of sitting in the seats or on the floor of a place of business as a means of protest.

strike The stopping of activities in protest or to get conditions met.

unconstitutional Unauthorized by the constitution of a country.

Index